RUTH HAIKUS

Steve Price

Printed in the United States
ISBN 9798737440602

This book is dedicated to my mother and all mothers,
wherever they may be.

TOO FAST

Whistling while she works—

all day long. At her age,

everything's work.

Her morning sneezes.

No one's counting.

The last one, a dud.

Couldn't hurt a fly.

They're too fast for her.

Bathes with Jean Naté,

Sprays her hair with Alberto.

Personal hygiene.

We'd lie on the couch
watching *General Hospital*.
Now the real thing.

Music therapist

sings us "Moon River".

My face is wet.

Her Thanksgiving tray.

She's not hungry.

Me neither.

Soundless morning.

I walk to her room, careful

not to step on a crack.

"When will this be over?"

She means the pandemic.

Coffee Häagen-Dazs,

single-serving cup.

She lets me feed her.

My phone rings.

She's gone.

Nachos on the table.

FROGS

Her frogs—

rings, pins, pendants—

a jump in my chest.

Another Sunday

without our Sunday phone call.

How long has it been?

It used to bug me—
questions, questions, questions!
Now I miss them.

Mother's Day coming up,

the first one without her.

I walk by the card store.

Indent balls of dough

with roundhead clothespin.

Fill with jelly.

Her purple watch

upon on my fingertips,

still telling time.

This winter, no box

of honey bell oranges.

Sun on our doorstep.

ALMOST

Snow-day trudge

to the store for cigarettes.

I lag behind her.

He's teaching tonight;

she takes me to Perkins.

Pancakes for supper!

R and P, her initials—

earrings from me

when I was ten.

Can any of these words

bring her back?

Almost.

"Hey Price, your mother!"

"At least I have a mother."

He points to her car.

Like an astronaut

walking a beagle on the moon.

Her snowmobile suit.

Ketzie: Yiddish

for kitten: how she signed

this note to my father.

Mad I stole the map,

she goes back and pays for it.

No one wants it.

She's tucking me in,

my face in her fur coat.

Saturday night.

All she wanted for me

was to be happy.

Here I go.